CW00504727

THE CANCER YEARS:

SOME ROUGH STUFF

ROLAND T WOODWARD

Copyrights © 2024 By

Roland T Woodward

All rights reserved. No part of this book may be reproduced or transmitted in any form by any means, electronic or mechanical, including photocopying and recording, or by any information storage and retrieval system, except as may be expressly permitted in writing from the author.

DEDICATION

This collection is dedicated to all those friends and colleagues who

have remained in contact and have supported me in my ongoing

battle with prostate cancer.

ABOUT THE AUTHOR

Roland Woodward is a retired chartered forensic psychologist. He is dyslexic and living in the United Kingdom, where he has written poetry all his life and has now found time to join other poets in his local area and to pursue publishing his poetry. Roland has previously published The Cancer Years: So Far, a collection of poems which were written during his ongoing battle with prostate cancer, which was diagnosed in 2019. He has also published The Travelling

Years a collection of poems written in English hotels and restaurants whilst traveling as a clinician and a third short collection, Herod's Children Crumulent Collection, a selection celebrating failure.

This collection The Cancer Years: Some Rough Stuff, is the second in the Cancer Years series that charts Roland's prostate cancer journey. It's a tricky path to chart as being in stage four with no cure available, it is not possible to judge accurately what will be the last in the Cancer Years series. All that can be hoped for is a long series.

Acknowledgment

I extend my heartfelt gratitude to WritersClique.com for publishing this book and a special thanks to Ted and Adam, my project managers, for their invaluable guidance. My editors, Anne and Shailene, deserve immense appreciation for their meticulous work and dedication. This book is a testament to the collective effort and talent of all involved.

I would like to acknowledge all those friends and colleagues who have written letters to me, WhatsApp messaged me and phoned me to encourage me and shared their thoughts over the last few difficult years. Their support has been greatly appreciated and given me strength to continue to fight and write. You know who you are, thank you, The Penguin, The Burton Group, Iron wife, Socky, Maximus, Drew the Blue Night, Judy, Di and Jo the Pageant Queen.

TABLE OF CONTENTS

363

I am scared,

and find myself shaking,

my body full of anxiety.

all my joints rigid, waiting,

the cancer is gnawing at,

body and soul.

For once, I am without options,

or strategy to cope.

I wanted to model death with dignity

but I find myself trembling,

breathless and terrified.

I tell myself the arithmetic is good,

and so it is, but it counts for nothing

when I piss blood

or my dick hurts afterward.

I take painkillers,

I take my meds

and try to rest,

my inactivity dampens me,

and I struggle to the surface

to gulp in air,

to pay attention

and to remain calm.

This is not what I had in mind,

a legacy of bravery for my family,

a model of how it can be done.

I fear I am failing in my last act,

the lines forgotten,

I am stumbling off the stage,

not exiting stage left

with a flourish and a kind word.

Writing this is a diversion,

a declaration of horror,

in on one last throw of the dice

to hold onto something.

How I envy Lawrence's bird

tumbling from its branch,

never feeling sorry for its self.

Nature made me different,

and it is a divide I cannot hide.

Of course, I will fight,

Of course, I will go on,

but I have no illusions anymore,

death is making me a coward.

So I may weep occasionally

and feel sorry for myself

as I feel the pull of earth and fire

and an end to it all.

363

6th January 2024

364

I've just seen myself,

I've been written down on a form,

"my terminally ill husband"

Just when I thought I was getting away with it.

Of course, I'm not stupid,

I know the score,

my bladder and my gut

tell me every day

it's getting worse.

Pain when I piss, sometimes,

unpredictable bowel movements,

it's all there,

written in the toilet,

where no one wants to go,

least of all me.

I was scared enough as it was,

but now my not so secret,

secret is out,

I'm terrified.

My drink of necessity is now hot water,

my food plain,

my hope draining away.

This is a terrible place to be,

I try to move and find I am pinned.

I flounder and thrash a little

as I try to see a poetry book through.

I try to fight, to see things happen,

to put up a good show,

but its miserable and

I can't help knowing it's going to get worse.

It's stark and bony

like my poetry,

like stepping from light to dark.

There is no argument to be had.

This is how it is,

and yet I want to fight,

to struggle and to go on.

It seems rude not to,

a betrayal of those who love me,

So just one more poem,

one more moment of trying

to capture the moment,

to be honest,

and to be alive.

Maybe, just maybe,

this is the side effect

of Chemo and twenty-eight day jabs,

but palliative means "sorry mate,

your fucked."

But pity me at your peril,

I have pen and ink

and in these, I have strength.

I am scared but not defeated,

I will fight,

I will find ways for little victories

before I go down,

I've not even reached

the morphine stage yet.

10-01-2024

365

I am distressed

by my search,

for a poem once read.

Indelible in my mind.

it spoke of the redundancy,

of consonance and assonance.

A Penguin Modern series,

of the sixties and seventies.

A man who wrote of prison,

the brutality of survival

and the way the blood flowed

when a man got shanked,

for him, that was poetry.

He was wrong,

for years in the heads

of the violent,

the killers,

the outcasts

there was only fear,

shame and loss.

When space allowed

there was wit and desire,

to be better.

I was never a therapist

more an operational moral philosopher,

just trying to find out

how to be a good person.

But the verses were always lodged,

ticking away in my mind

that there is something,

beyond the structure

and the academic noun.

A depth beyond

the contrivances and the intricacies.

I'm running out of time

and have no space for the fripperies,

or linguistic baubles,

if I am to find

what lies at the heart

of the words that move

the world of being.

My dandelion clock

sheds itself

as the wind blows,

and still, I seek

the lost poem

and the ones to come.

23-01-24.

(William Wantling, poetry. Found it!)

366

I can't do this,

I've panicked.

I got into the changing room

And things changed.

So many people,

no privacy,

I can't face this.

I retreat

to the lounge.

Is this how I am now?

Scared to share

a space,

the sight of my body,

the length of my hair,

my reduced state.

Hot chocolate

ordered and runaway with.

I tip-tap on my phone,

hoping the Dementors leave.

I sip at my cup, hopefully.t

I wait for my partner

to rescue me.

The gym, once a haven

is now a bear pit of vulnerability,

The teeth and

claws of death everywhere.

Another toke of chocolate

another line,

Perhaps this is how I survive.

Out here requires energy,

and I am spoonless.

I feel stupid,

weak and a freak,

most of all, I am alone,

in the worst possible place.

The voice inside says

"self-pitying bastard."

and I cringe from myself.

No amount of arithmetic

and vitals being right

makes it go away.

I smile as I realise

I do not know how to keep this.

No idea how I can end this,

I'm scared.

28-01-2024

David Lloyd Gym.

367

I know people think

that I'm getting on with life,

I'm not.

There is an assumption,

that I am okay,

I'm not.

My blog suggests,

that I am coping,

I am not.

The silence implies

I am fine,

I am not.

The Real World is too busy

to notice,

I am not.

It's scary,

That's what.

12th February 2024

368

I have meditation in my ears

where once was Ginsberg,

that howling man of America,

seeing lions and decrying

the loss of self.

I heard the voice

of stand-up poetry,

the passion and the humour,

compassion for the other.

How and where does it come from,

these tears unshed, this despair?

There in the air is the message

that I shall never,

or never shall,

speak aloud

this distress contained within.

Slowly but surely, disintegration

seeps through both body and being

that is unspeakable

to a world of war and

others' pain and burdens.

This utter insignificance

is desert-like in its vastness.

I have visions, fantasies

of knowing rest

but it is all too much.

I turn up the volume

of Alexa's calming offerings.

Noises, not music, supposedly serene

but now wallpaper to hang around me,

buying time to write;

no; scribble, scratch around

the fear of dying.

As things slow down

I function less.

Every blog starts

with the word "fight."

but my jabs are slow,

my hooks weak,

all from memory

of who I used to be.

What I am now is too terrifying

to look at, freakish,

a thing I never thought I would be.

Not just old but dying

beyond my control,

like this poem

it is too long, drawn-out

and never a hint

of Ginsberg, Wantling, Ferlingheti

and all the breathless poets whose voices

shook the world.

All I ever was is

never to be.

Ungrammatical silence is my legacy.

368

14th February 2024

369

I used to read to my children

Tommy Tin Can,

"If anyone can, Tommy Tin Can can".

To this day they can

do the Tommy can can.

Now my story is different,

and it is Prost8kancerman.

If I can, Prost8kancerman can.

When I do, Prost8kancerman does,

and is chronicled in the blog

videoed on his YouTube channel.

So, from stories for children

it's stories for me

to reassure I still can.

369 02-03-2024

370

Abbey was her name,

perky, smiley from 111.

A paramedic to assess me

after I could stand

the blood no more.

In dusty pink scrubs

she listens, takes cyber notes

and examines vitals.

Her hands are cold,

her smile broad.

She has read my file

And shared what others haven't.

She seems surprised

that the truth has been a secret.

She explains her explanation

for the bloody sample

and prescribes.

We have a strategy,

this is how medicine should be,

even on a Sunday.

She leaves

and I fight on.

That's one hell of a paramedic

and I am not sure I said thank you.

370

02-03-2024

371

I know it's not like the real thing;

that I am a pretender in the game

but holding my first book

I feel joy.

in all this losing poetry

is my history,

the bits my family

never got to see it.

All those nooks and crannies

and other constructs

of my universe.

With time running out

it's a route to get inside out

so that my children know

who I am.

371

11-03-2024

37²

God bless America,

and its Eastern Standard Time,

lagging languidly behind

my beloved Greenwich Mean Time.

God bless America,

and its Writer Clique,

with a hard sell,

"give us your money,

we don't care if it's shit."

attitude publishing company.

God bless America,

for it's can-do doing things,

it's strange accents

and taking my money.

God bless America

for its greenback dollar bills

smaller than my Great British Pounds,

but in this paper, we trust,

one to make them rich

and one to make me immortal.

God bless America

With its crazy Z's

Where my beloved S's sit.

All those cross-cultural snippets

of adaption and ignorance.

God bless America

for publishing my collection

and setting it free

on Universal Amazon.

God bless America

With its chaos,

its bewildering kaleidoscope

that Rule Britannia seems pleased

to mimic, ape and applaud.

God bless America

For not noticing

that I have slipped in,

got over the border wall

like a boat person

over the English Channel.

I am now in black and white

And it feels good.

God bless America.

372

13-03-2024

373

I made it,

there is cherry blossom,

a Japanese book

by my side.

Orange squash and biscuits

alongside me on the

recliner.

So here is Spring,

pots full of bulbs

and waving yellow

trumpets to fanfare

the fact that

I am still

here.

The heating is off

and vests redundant.

Life unwrapped nods
and summer beckons,
tempting me to spend
spoons I have not
got.

373

19-03-2024

374

I never saw you so broken

she said amidst the tears.

Me huddled in the front seat

going home from the

aborted luxury break.

I never made it

to the first night,

bladder saw to that.

Ever twenty minutes

of painful pissing,

banging my head on the wall,

pleading with my dick

to stop hurting me.

Once again, I throw myself

On the mercy of my doctor.

He reads my last scan report,

Oh he says

You have a large bladder stone.

The oncologist boys

 must have missed it,

they only read the summary.

So now it's back to urology

To see their "stone" man.

Now I have enough co-codamol

to lay an elephant low,

a new pissing chart

and pain scale record.

"I never saw you so broken"

I have never been so guilty

Distressed and ashamed

that I have so disappointed

my partner.

What weight have I added

to an already heavy burden.

The anxiety of death runs wild,

and the realisation

there is no good end

to this bites deeply.

This is a bad time

where everyone is scared

and wondering where the strength

to carry on will come from.

"I've never seen you so broken"

I understand how the burden

weighs now

and how not being,

like Naruda's luckless slinger

found everything sank in you

and your

"I've never seen you so broken,"

374

28-03-2024

375

My Cancer Years: So Far

remain mute in my family's mouths.

Too painful to read

and certainly beyond discussion.

In my effort to share

and to put into the world

the experience of my gnawing companion,

I reap silence.

Like all my Herod's children

they have been submitted

and only elicited the acknowledgment

of effort and the insubstantiality

of their content.

This is how my family

protects itself from my inner world,

the Dark and Tricky battlefield

in which Rocket and I

wage war,

to die fighting

with our pride intact.

The pain is not for hearing,

hope needs something else

other than a bare honesty

that plunges my kin into loss

and death before I am gone.

I never tried to hurt them

only to explain

but the unbearable

has won out.

There is a limit

to how much I can contain,

so my cancerous self

continues to spill

onto the page

but with no expectation

other than execution .

375

04-04-2024

376

I've got a bladder stone,

two point two

by one point two centimeters.

I've seen it on the scans,

you could spot it from space.

My first thought:

"That's fucking huge!"

followed quickly by

"that's going to hurt".

The doctor chap explains,

"we can smash it up",

and once again I think:

"that's going to hurt a lot".

Back at home, I am

wondering just how long

is the waiting list

for the demolition.

I decide to make friends

but chums need names

so I cast around for something benign.

There are several candidates,

Watts after the rolling stone,

Sisyphus, plagued by his rock,

Wayne after "The Rock" Johnson.

None feel right.

Perhaps Eric after the girl's pet rock

in "What we did on our Holiday."

Finally I have it.

Uluru,

After all it is a rock down under.

It made me smile,

and pals are supposed to do that.

376

04-04-2024

377

My eyes defocus and I am left

awash on the waves of a cornfield of sound.

Standing in a pack of people all talking in that good time way.

Louder and louder, it grows as I sink beneath its tides,

it is unbearable as on it sweeps, building into an ocean that drowns

me.

Cacophony fills me as I falter, desperate not to hear, to be struck

deaf to this babbling;

I retreat to the toilets.

Sitting there in an oasis of ordinary silence,

interrupted only by the occasional occupant's coughs and farts

I find respite.

If I am to dine and participate in this nights entertainment

I must return to the cauldron.

Sitting at table seven, trying to make conversation with nice people,

the pain continues.

Over breakfast, a couple come and apologise for being quiet

for they too were deafened by humanity out for a jolly time.

I know what purgatory is now.

377

07-04-2024

378

Everywhere I turn there are gems

lying on the literary sands,

mined from the universes of others.

Friends send me gifts,

always books

and so my library grows.

My eyes open anew

as each finely cut jewel

dazzles me.

I'm blinded by the brightness

and invention with which

others find the words

that capture those places

inside me that I strive

to find expression for.

378 09-04-2024

National Unicorn Day

379

Bits of me lost forever
tucked away somewhere
or shredded.
All were gifts,
unsolicited and unexpected,
so it should be no surprise
that no trace remains.
They are moments of
honour or affection
that have escaped a number.
Those impulses let loose
to find their own way
to mind or heart,
to carry a message that the conversation
could not contain.
Moments of awe
when the internal universe
was shaken to its core,
when the self was overwhelmed
and the iron wife
smiled in recognition.
There have been mirrors,
brush strokes

but all of them gone
now, as I number
and put my life in order
I miss them.
They are the words
By which people knew me,
of what stirred inside
and could not be contained.
Magic moments, spilled
and given over.
There can never be
a complete work,
only the body
that I have clung to
only for it to turn upon me
and see me incomplete.

379
09-04-2024
Unicorn Day.

380

Did I or didn't I

take the paracetamol?

Something distracted me

and I am paranoid about more

so I recline and close my eyes,

perhaps sleep will move

this headache.

It sounds serious

this memory glitch,

perhaps madness and senility

are poking fingers

into sulci and gyri,

or am I just getting old?

Dyslexia accounts for the names

but this is something else,

a preoccupation to stay

engaged

brings bright, shiny things,

a dazzling array

of thoughts.

It is a quandary

that a nap and this poem

has dispelled.

I can always do co-codamol;

or can I?

380

11-04-2024

381

I do not cry,

I am not given to

lachrymose out pouring's,

the tear duct flood

of weepiness.

No, I sternly

look for solutions

and moving on.

It is true I am dry;

except;

Opera!

Opera makes me tearful,

Carmen and her cards,

Cio-Cio San's second act

lament of hope,

Callas's Tosca

and the tragedy of Grimes,

all of these reduce me

beyond my control.

Even Freddie and Monserrat

pierce me.

It is the sound of

 song so high that

rips through me

and trips the switch

for which I have

no defence.

I have no idea why,

all I can do

is surrender totally,

in wonder

and hope there

is more to come

for in those moments

I might just believe

I have true kindness in me.

381

11-04-2024

382

I sit and wait

to see if I am all right.

I've been to the loo,

that's always a tricky time,

bloody? Stingy? Easy?

It is the dipstick

of my well-being.

The most natural of functions

becomes the barometer

of my being.

Basic, brutal and barbaric

but all I have to gauge

how the war is going.

So I sit and let myself settle

listening in my head to

Under Milk Wood

and that landscape of words

caped in dark and black

which flows in a dream world

of the imagined every day

of buggerall.

Its alliteration soothes me

and calms my troubled

self until I am able to

engage again.

I think I am okay

until I spot

Butcher Beynon walking

down the road,

a finger in his mouth,

not his own.

383

17-04-2024

383

This is a bad day
after a poor night.
I've no energy at all
and everything is an effort.
I struggled to recall Ginsberg
and even more so Clematis.
As my tongue twists
around the subdued synapse.
I don't know why this occurs,
it springs like a wolf
sensing a lamb in trouble.
Co-codamol tempts me
but it's a coward's way out.
I seek solace
by reclining with TV
and a mindless hope
for peace and quiet,
both in and out.

1st April 2024.

384

This sheet is waiting

like a conductor's baton.

The hand that holds the pen

frozen in an icy lock.

Surrounded by painted glass,

half-finished quarter boards,

scribbled notes for books,

friend's art and wax;

the jewellery yet to be caste.

But at this moment,

nothing, a desert of blankness.

So, this page waits

like an act of faith,

and equally illogical.

The wall is a question,

who do I trust enough

to be the executor of my Will.

I know the nooks and crannies

of people too well

to assume that death

cleans the soul

and makes others honest,

unbendable and true.

A puppet for the hand

of death.

9TH August 2023

385

It's a new life style,

drive there,

sit there,

drive back.

Its containment

of this wicked disease.

Life has become a series

of short episodes of entertainment

and contact beyond the family.

Each trip holds risks

but the harvest is a feast

of food for the brain

as life stops being physical

and becomes cerebral.

Once a month I wrap myself

in poets.

Their words and reading

the best of food,

the discussion the sweetest source.

It is this dining

that fattens me

and sees me through

the lean times.

In between courses

friends send me books

so my feet up recoveries

are picnics, sometimes snacks.

This is how I outwait

the waiting lists,

the endless English queuing

politely understanding the pressures

and the fact that everyone

is trying their best.

So here I lay

browsing and grazing

hankering after a rowing machine

and clear urine

to reassure me

that I can stretch

the survival

curve.

385

27-04-2024

386

I am trying really hard

not to be a nuisance,

endeavouring not to add

to the general pain.

Every way I turn, those I love

are battling oceans of storms.

It is as if the world

has filled itself with illness

without cure or palliative care.

I really am trying

but its hard to deny my decline,

those subtle, sore signs

that things are getting worse.

My head weaves benign explanations,

makes up logical explanations

for this and that

ache and ague,

each difficulty and soreness,

but deep down, I know

I'm on a slippery slope.

I tell myself that this is

a negative mindset,

that I am making things worse,

that being chipper and upbeat

would help, but I know it's not true.

I've either been or being ground

fine in the grindstones of my disease

and finally, it's found its way

to bring me down.

I really am trying

to be brave and not cause a fuss,

I'd just like a hug,

but so would everyone else

in the midst of their travails.

It's a busy world of pain

And there is no time

to stop, just rest when opportunity arises

and then start all over again.

I realise we are all trying hard

and the silence of my loved ones
is a different kind of unbearable,
a mute gagging on the expected
loss and perception of the ebbing
flow from those they love.
I'm trying really hard
in my way to carry on,
but the mirrors I look into
show me failure, decline, and
worst of all, the aloneness.
No one else but me can do this,
this standing, looking over
the landscape of my life
and putting away my feelings
knowing there is not enough
care or love to take away or slay
this singularity.
I am trying really hard
not to be a miserable old git,
the downer in everyone's day,
the grandfather and father

who is no fun anymore,

just the old guy who has to be asked,

"Are you okay"?

I miss being loved,

I miss the no strings attached affection,

the delight in me,

like some immortal,

an everlasting thing of joy.

A shiny object with a future

and more fun to come.

The Real World swallows us whole

and love becomes duty,

obligation and a chore,

a world devoid of its core.

Is this depression,

is this the manifestation

of some chemical imbalance

or is this life in its later form?

I do not know

but I'm trying really hard.

Trying really hard to be okay,

to ignore my longings and to

get on.

To that end, I'll take the drugs

and hope at least the pain subsides

long enough to give another hug.

I'm trying really hard.

Perhaps my next collection will be called

"Self-Pitying Bastard"

I think I'm trying really hard,

perhaps I'm not;

not hard enough.

386

04-05-2024

Printed in Great Britain
by Amazon

45988310R00036